What Weighs 70,000 Pounds and **Swallows Stones?**

WRITTEN BY **Robert Kanner**

ILLUSTRATED BY **Russ Daff**

dingles & company New Jersey

FOR ELLIOT, LYNN, JACLYN, AND JAMIE

First Printing

Published by dingles&company
P.O. Box 508
Sea Girt, New Jersey 08750

**LIBRARY OF CONGRESS
CATALOG CARD NUMBER**
2007904356

ISBN
978-1-59646-840-5

Printed in the United States
of America

The Uncover & Discover series is
based on the original concept
of Judy Mazzeo Zocchi.

ART DIRECTION & DESIGN
Rizco Design

EDITORIAL CONSULTANT
Andrea Curley

PROJECT MANAGER
Lisa Aldorasi

EDUCATIONAL CONSULTANTS
Melissa Oster and Margaret Bergin

CREATIVE DIRECTOR
Barbie Lambert

PRE-PRESS
Pixel Graphics

WEBSITE
www.dingles.com

E-MAIL
info@dingles.com

The Uncover & Discover series encourages children to inquire, investigate, and use their imagination in an interactive and entertaining manner. This series helps to sharpen their powers of observation, improve reading and writing skills, and apply knowledge across the curriculum.

Uncover each one and see you can when you're

clue one by what dinosaur discover done!

My 2-foot-long **head**
is very small compared
to my huge body. I hold it
straight out and parallel
to the ground.

WHERE IS THE **HEAD**?

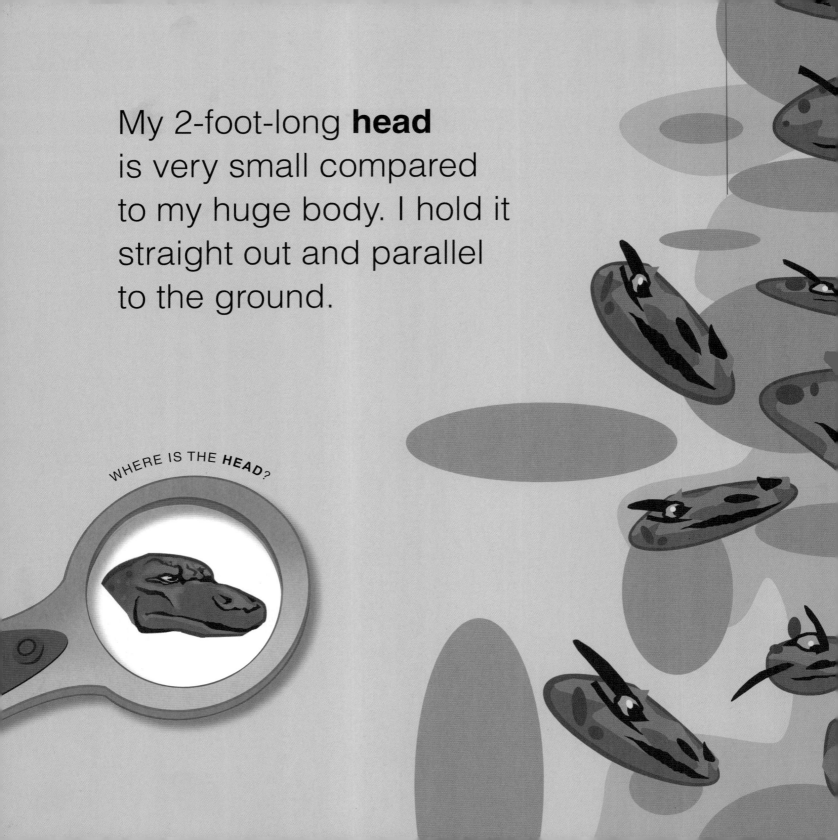

My **eyes** are located
toward the top of my head.

LOOK FOR THE **EYE**.

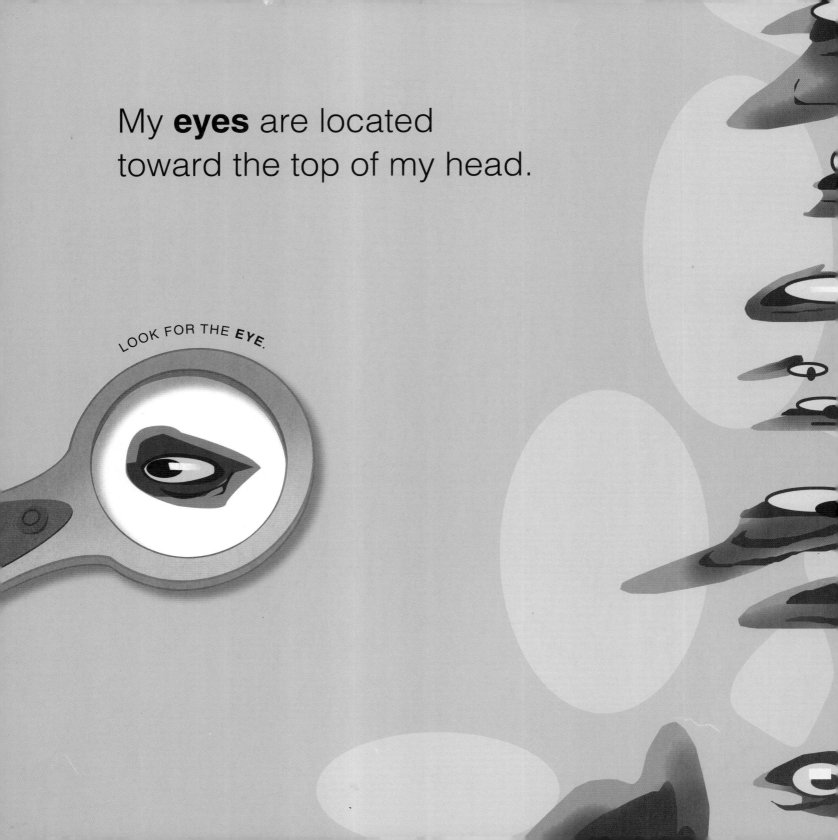

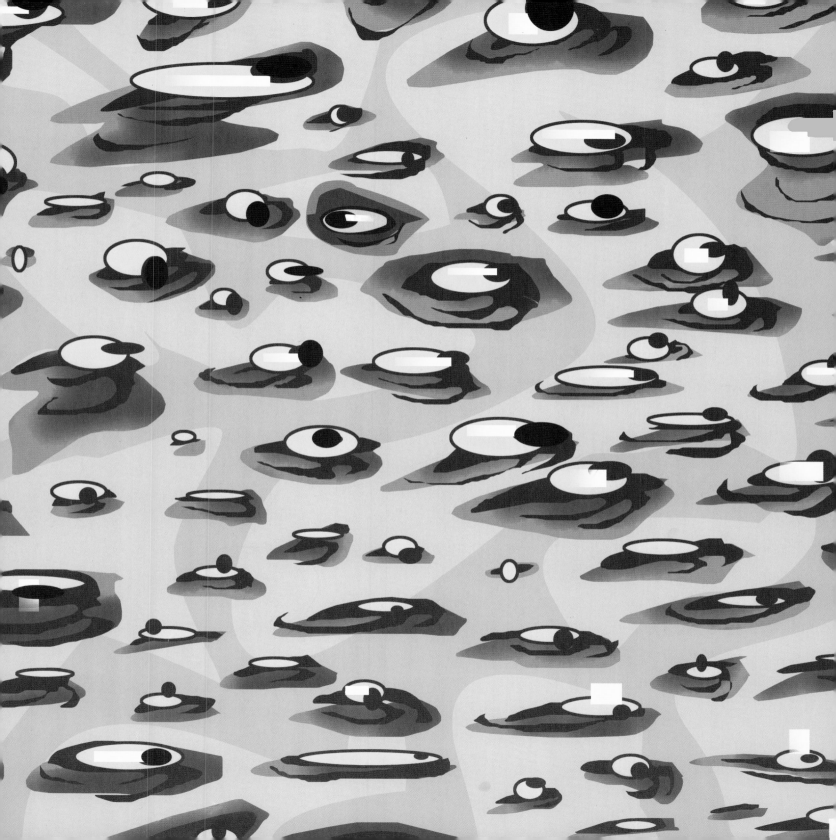

My large **nostrils**
are on top of my snout.

FIND THE **NOSTRILS**.

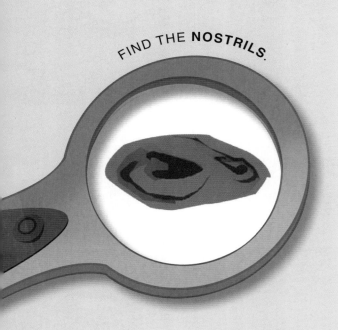

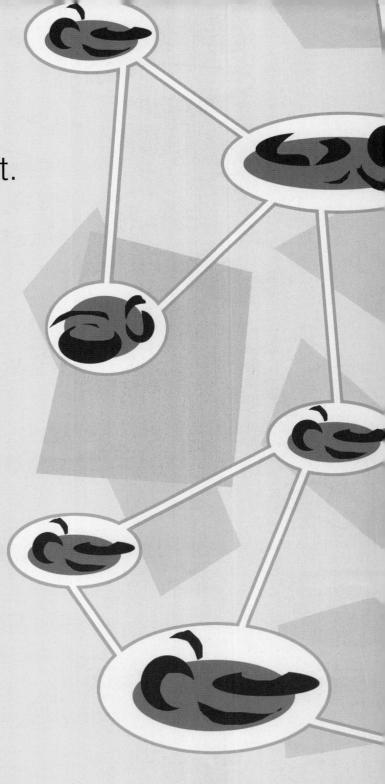

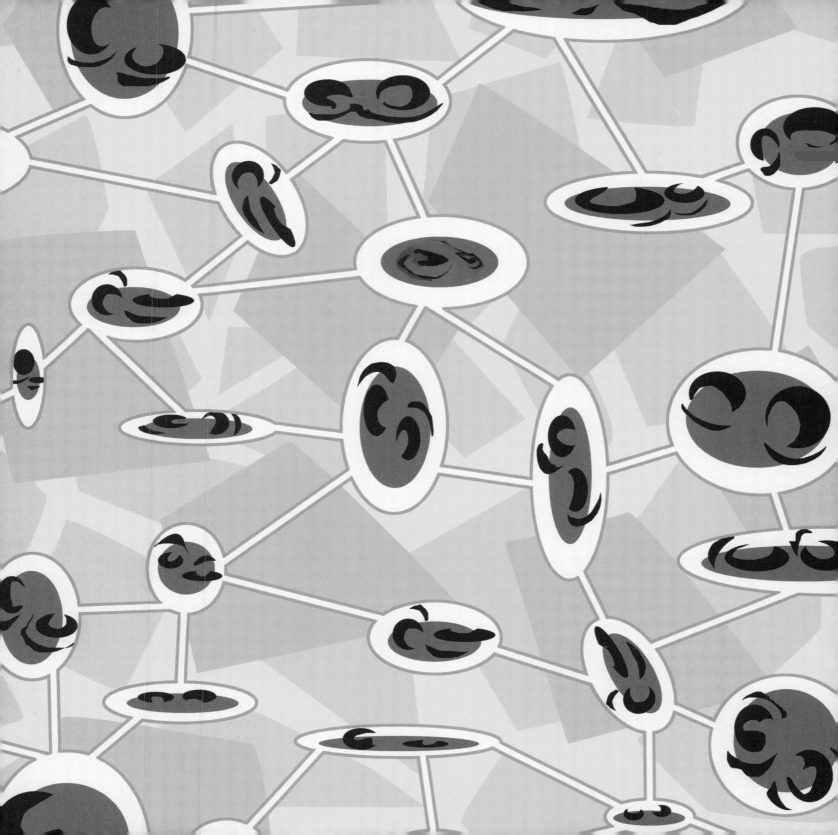

I use my 20-foot-long **neck** to poke my head into the trees to find the leaves that I eat.

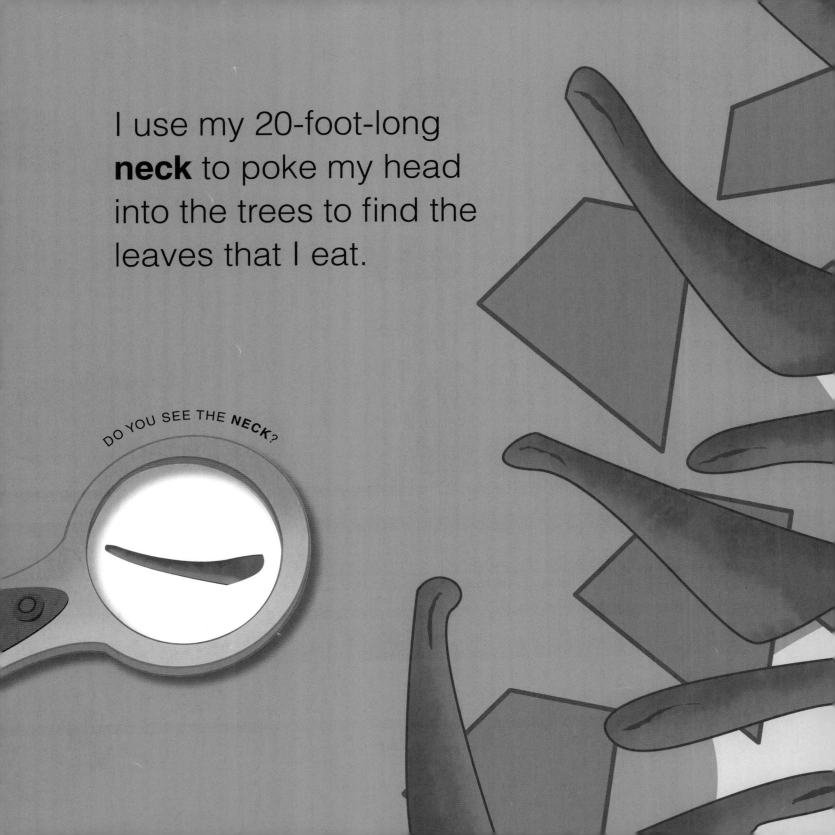

DO YOU SEE THE **NECK**?

Swinging my neck from side to side helps me to find low-lying plants such as **ferns** that I also eat.

WHERE IS THE **FERN?**

My **mouth** is small, so I have to eat all the time in order to feed my extremely large body.

LOOK FOR THE **MOUTH**.

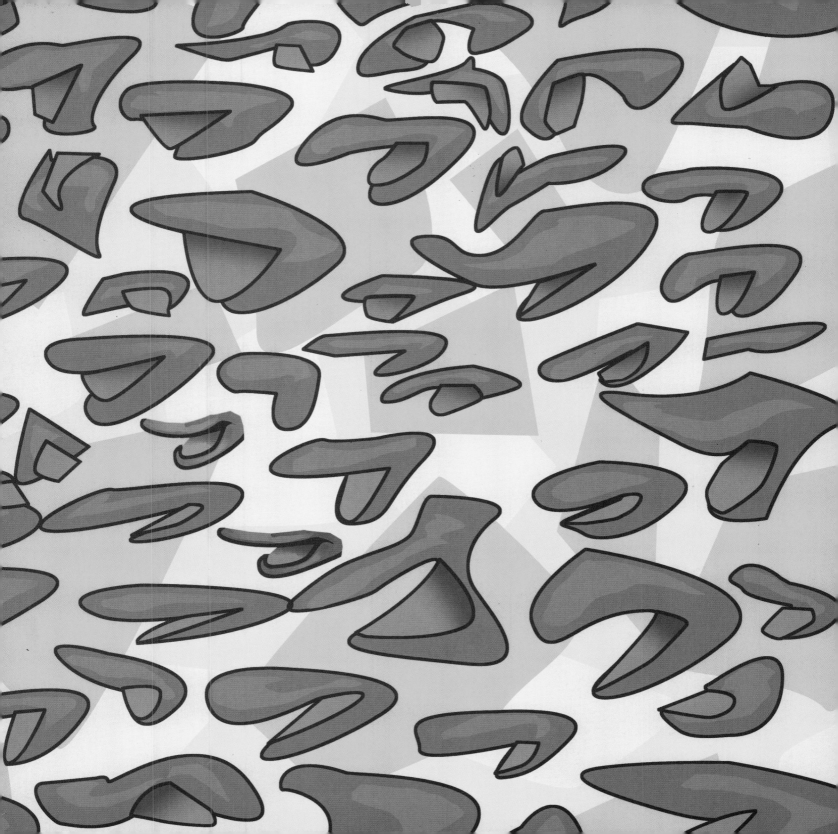

I have cylinder-shaped **teeth** at the front of my jaw. I use them to strip the leaves off the branches and plants that I eat.

FIND THE **TEETH**.

I eat **stones** to grind
up the tough plants in
my stomach because
I swallow my food whole.

DO YOU SEE THE **STONES?**

I walk slowly on my four thick, pole-shaped **legs**.

WHERE IS THE **LEG**?

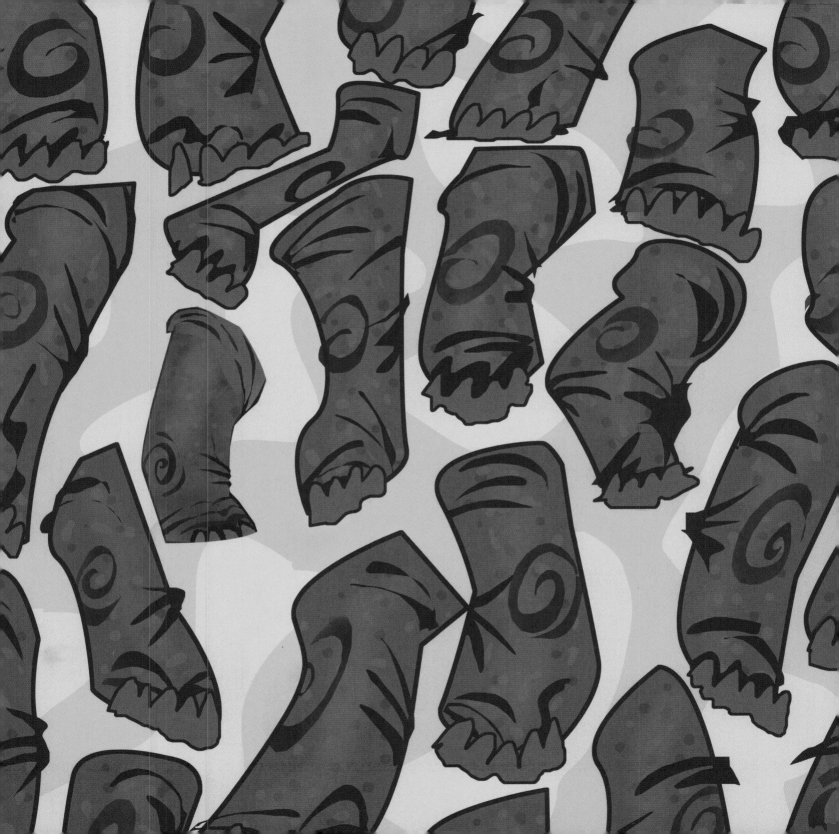

My **feet** are about
36 inches wide.

LOOK FOR THE **FOOT**.

A large **claw** on each front foot helps me defend myself from enemies.

FIND THE **CLAW**.

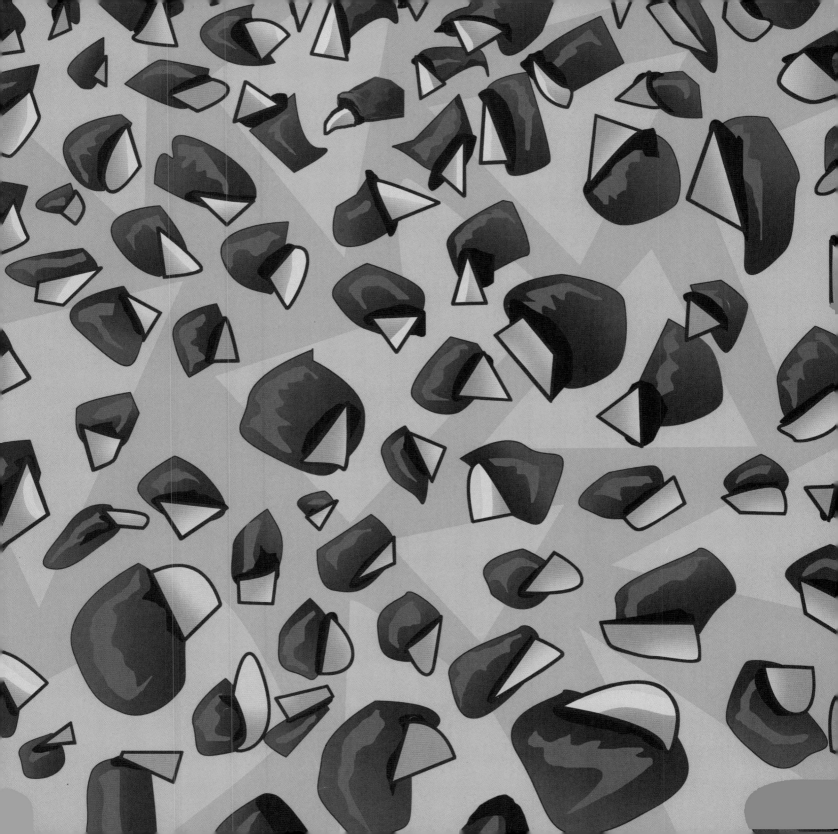

When I swing my long neck, my 30-foot-long **tail** helps me to keep my balance. I also use my strong tail to defend myself.

DO YOU SEE THE **TAIL**?

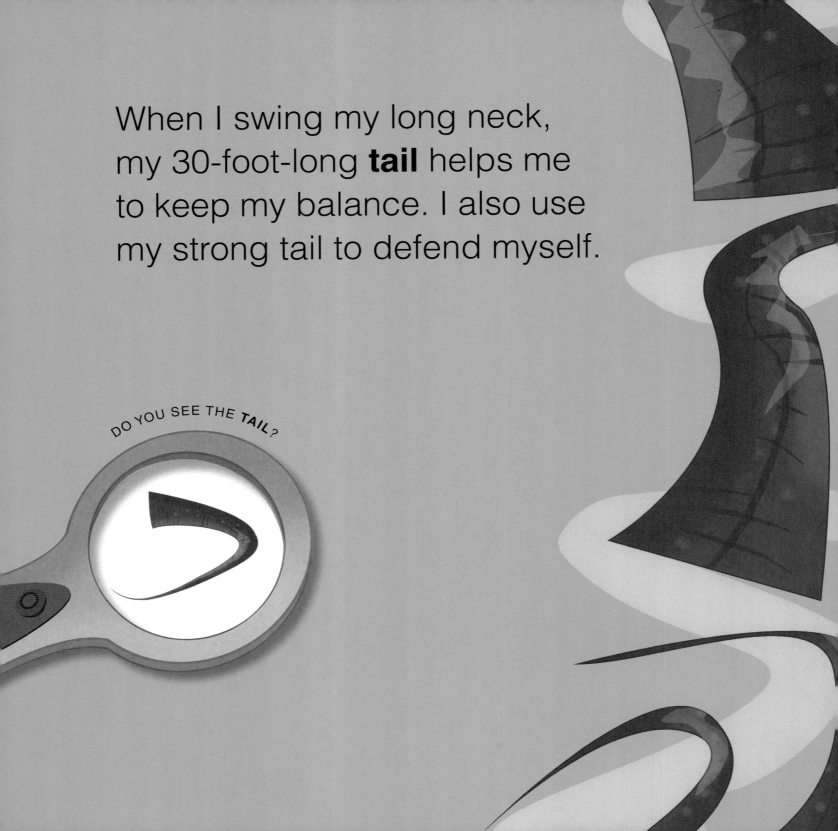

You have uncovered the clues. **Have you guessed what I am?**

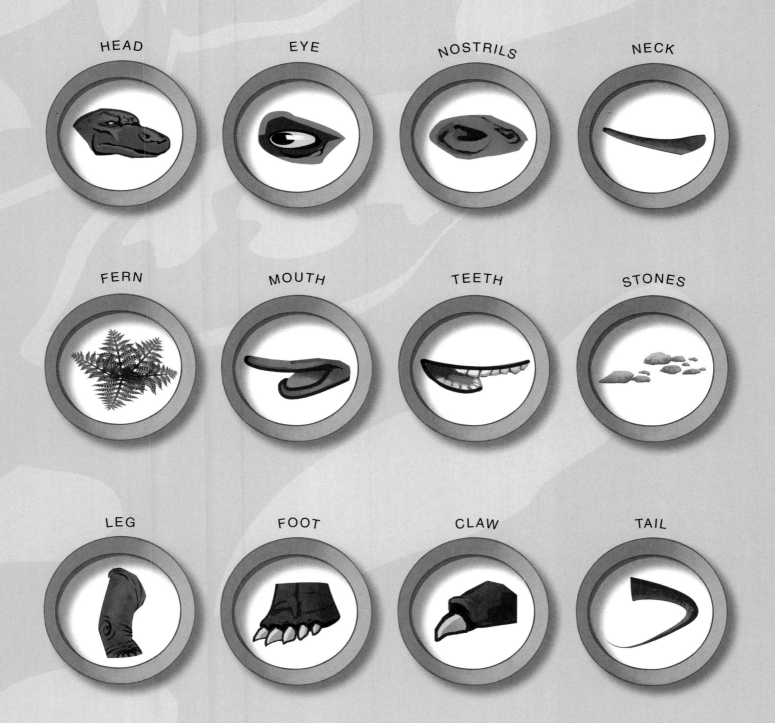

HEAD

EYE

NOSTRILS

NECK

FERN

MOUTH

TEETH

STONES

LEG

FOOT

CLAW

TAIL

If not, here are more clues...

1. I am a prehistoric reptile that lives on the land.

2. I am one of a group of four-legged dinosaurs that are the largest land animals that ever existed. We have very long necks, small heads with blunt teeth, and long tails.

3. My head is about 2 feet long (about the size of a horse's head). My brain is about the size of an apple.

4. I am about 80 feet long (the length of almost three school buses lined up in a row!) and about 15 feet tall.

weigh around 70,000 pounds, about the same weight as seven elephants tied together.

walk very, very slowly because my legs are stiff and have limited movement. They are built mainly to hold up my weight and keep me balanced.

hatched from a very large egg, almost a foot wide.

live in a region that is now in the western United States.

am a herbivore, which means I eat plants.

Now add them up and you'll see...

Do you want to know more about me? Here are some *Apatosaurus* fun facts.

1. *Apatosaurus* (a-pat-oh-SAWR-us) means "deceptive lizard." It was named this because it was similar to other plant-eating dinosaurs with thick, five-toed legs ("lizard-footed"); long necks; small brains; and long tails.

2. *Apatosaurus* lived during the late Jurassic period, about 150 million years ago. During this period what was once a huge landmass had separated into continents. This is the period when dinosaurs such as gigantic plant eaters and smaller meat eaters roamed the land.

3. *Apatosaurus* eggs were found in a line, not in a nest. Scientists believe that the eggs were laid as the mother dinosaur was walking and that she did not take care of her eggs.

4. *Apatosaurus* toes were short, wide, and blunt. A large, straight claw on each front foot helped the dinosaur grip the ground when moving forward.

5. The only dinosaur of the time that could attack *Apatosaurus* was the 30-foot-long *Allosaurus*. Scientists know this because teeth marks of this ferocious meat eater were found in the fossil bones of an apatosaurus.

6. An apatosaurus probably would have lived for about 100 years.

7. *Apatosaurus* was named by Othniel C. Marsh, a paleontologist (a scientist who learns about prehistoric life-forms by studying fossils), in 1877. He discovered the first fossil in Colorado. A few years later he discovered another fossil and named this dinosaur *Brontosaurus*. However, it turned out that the two dinosaurs were actually two different members of the same group of dinosaurs—*Apatosaurus*.

Who, What, Where, When, Why, and How

USE THE QUESTIONS who, what, where, when, why, and how to help the child apply knowledge and process the information in the book. Encourage him or her to investigate, inquire, and imagine.

In the Book...

DO YOU KNOW WHO named *Apatosaurus*?

DO YOU KNOW WHAT the featured dinosaur in the book is?

DO YOU KNOW WHERE the first *Apatosaurus* fossil was found?

DO YOU KNOW WHEN *Apatosaurus* lived?

DO YOU KNOW WHY *Apatosaurus* ate stones?

DO YOU KNOW HOW big *Apatosaurus*'s head was?

In Your Life...

The next time you see 3 school buses lined up in a row in front of your school at dismissal time, just think: That's how long *Apatosaurus* was!

CROSS-CURRICULAR EXTENSIONS

Math

An apatosaurus eats 2 groups of plants with 20 plants in each group. The apatosaurus then eats 9 large plants and 3 small plants. How many plants did the apatosaurus eat in all?

Science

Which was the only dinosaur that was able to attack *Apatosaurus*? How do scientists know this?

Social Studies

In order to become a paleontologist (a scientist who learns about life-forms in prehistoric times by studying fossils), what school subjects do you think you would have to do well in? Why?

Fun Activity

You have uncovered the clues and discovered *Apatosaurus*.

ASSIGNMENT

Write a funny dinosaur story. Imagine a comical situation that an apatosaurus has gotten into.

INCLUDE IN YOUR STORY

Who are the characters in the story?
What are they doing that is funny?
Where does the story take place?
When does the story take place—in prehistoric times or in the present day?
Why is the apatosaurus in this situation?
How does the story end?

WRITE

Enjoy the writing process while you take what you have imagined and create your funny story.

UNCOVER &DISCOVER

Author

Robert Kanner is part of the writing team for the Uncover & Discover series as well as the Global Adventures and Holiday Happenings series. An extensive career in the film and television business includes work as a film acquisition executive at the Walt Disney Company, a story editor for a children's television series, and an independent family-film producer. He holds a bachelor's degree in psychology from the University of Buffalo and lives in the Hollywood Hills, California, with Tom and Miss Murphy May.

Illustrator

Since graduating from Falmouth School of Art in 1993, **Russ Daff** has enjoyed a varied career. For eight years he worked on numerous projects in the computer games industry, producing titles for Sony PlayStation and PC formats. While designing a wide range of characters and environments for these games, he developed a strong sense of visual impact that he later utilized in his illustration and comic work. Russ now concentrates on his illustration and cartooning full-time. When he is not working, he enjoys painting, writing cartoon stories, and playing bass guitar. He lives in Cambridge, England.